Dawn-light

Dawn-light

INSCAPE, LOVE REFLEX, ECHOES OF OTHER VOICES AND
MOMENTS OF PERSONAL CLARITY 1964-2014

M. C. REITZ

*Dawn-light: Inscape, Love Reflex, Echoes of Other Voices
and Moments of Personal Clarity 1964-2014*

By M.C. Reitz

ISBN 978-602-8397-00-1

Printed in the United States

For all those who birthed some part of my world assisting me in authoring my own life.

Contents

Dawn-light

Dawn
when the power, the energy, the light rays, the Sun
You pierce the darkness,
flood the heavens,
burn off the haze, the fog, the blurred vision
of dew wet clouds.
Pierce me, flow over me, enlighten me
to the way of Dawn,
the way of life,
the path beneath the trees,
the over the mountain pass,
the path that circles globe earth,
the path into the universe,
the path into my mind – my head beyond the skull
where dawn-light and I are one.

Beyond hurried, beyond cluttered,
beyond jammed, crammed,
beyond beeping, honking, chatting,
beyond the noise, the clashing, the thrashing of cement
and steel,
yapping mouths fighting and arguing, beating nerves to
death.

Dawn, pierce me, flow over me, enlighten me
where dawn-light and I are one.

A Little Salt

I'm smart enough to discuss many subjects
but not smart enough to be certain.
I'm smart enough to help my neighbor
but not smart enough to help the world.
I'm smart enough to know right from wrong
but not smart enough to know who is guilty.
I'm smart enough to feed my family
but not smart enough to become rich.
I'm smart enough to direct my own life
but not smart enough to direct others.
I'm smart enough to know that there is a God
but not smart enough to distinguish among religions.
I live my life a little smart and a little ignorant,
a little right and a little wrong.
Unable to be big, I am little.
Can a little go a long way?
Is a little salt enough to flavor the soup?

Life Enough

Fresh air is inhalant enough.

Fresh water is liquid enough.

Fruit, vegetables & grains are food enough.

Old threads are clothes enough.

Good legs are transportation enough.

Any shelter is home enough.

Friends are entertainment enough.

This moment is time enough.

Carpenter's Song

The woodpile gone now,

 design has no room for odd waste.

When I was a boy

sitting afield

fingering scraps of wood for burning,

feeling power to love

even the unwanted pieces.

Two Stones at Risk

I hold two stones,

one in each hand, and

toss them into the air.

I fumble one or the other or both

as they fall to the ground.

If I keep them in my sweaty hands,

I never have any fun…

The Window

Take your chances
with the air currents,
the flying things,
the crawly things,
the sounds of forest talk,
and the dark.
Stick your head out,
look and see,
what has been plowed under
flourishes again...
fresh air, fresh scents,
fresh fruitful rain
soaking mother earth.
Turn off the control knobs,
still the machines,
leave behind the reasoned institutions.
Enjoy...even for a moment,
in silence,
the intuitions of the soul.

Pioneer

I am not a pioneer

but I am willing to take the road less traveled

I am not a leader

but I am willing to forge on when others are afraid

I am not a man of caution

but I am willing to stop when everyone else is

rushing forward...

Easter Sunrise

Directed to a window seat
An overlook of the intersection of streets
With a beer and empty of thought
My eyes see and yet do not understand
The colorful motion of people and vehicles below
At a corner table two men sit
A point synchronized with the confluence of streets
The thin, smallish, mustached, light-haired Swede, Ulf,
Held the questions of the younger chub-faced London
truck driver.
From somewhere beneath the table
A portfolio of large colorful prints appeared
One at a time the Swede shared them with the Brit
With a twinkle in his eye, he noticed my eavesdropping
And handed the pictures to me
At this moment: Why me? Why India? Why Mcleod Ganj?
Why these photos? Why this beer?
Why this mystery of the street below?
What is it to me?
Exquisite photos they were
Of women and children
Planted with the earth
At one with the shocks of grain in the field
At one with the adobe walls of their homes
At one with one another
Familiar and yet foreign to me

At this confluence of earth energy, Ulf and I sat
together
Luke, an ex-addict from London on a journey of self
Frank from Alaska penniless and volunteering his
computer skills and his life
Rita, the surgical nurse from Vancouver

Attila the Turk, and the young Tibetan woman
All came to sit a spell with Ulf
Six or seven laughing and talking
As I excused myself
The '80s brought Ulf here to photograph and meditate
A few rupees here and there sufficient for body and
soul
Ulf hypothesized that this very spot on which we sat
To be the most international place on earth
He triggered within me a vision
Light rays and energy emanating from this place,
McLeod Ganj
Touching around the earth
Then I knew why
Why I was here
Why so many have come and gone
Attaching themselves to the awakening
Taking it home. The sun rises with us
Where ever we are on earth.

The Loving Kindness of Krishna, Buddha, the
Christ and the Others
Help us find our true selves.

Small Incidents in India

A back alley in Delhi,
children shout from above,
"Dadaji! Dadaji! Dadaji!"
I look up to see
four young children
leaning over
a third floor balcony
pointing at me,
joy in their eyes.
I smile and wave
as they shower me
with laughter.
My Sikh friend, Vicky,
walks up the alley
from the other way.
"What do they say?" I ask.
"Grandfather, Grandfather,"
he shouts with a broad smile.
At that moment
I feel at home
in India.

"Wait" my Indian friend says,
"Do not eat now!"
We will cook Indian spicy food

for you to eat later with us,
the same food that we eat.
I feel at home
in India.

The first time
I entered
the small Tibetan shop,
I noticed the quiet calm.
The woman behind the counter
said nothing.
She simply looked up
with the gift
of her smile.
I came to that shop often
to see her child
to meet her grandpa
to enjoy her smile.
I felt at home
in India.

Raja and I
sat on the porch in the evening
overlooking the Kangra Valley
with the spread of the Milky Way
beyond our reach;
yet, not beyond our imagination.
Raja fingered intricate patterns

coaxing his guitar into soulful rhythms.
We smoked and talked
of stars and earth,
our spacious dream
for all mankind.
I felt at home
in India.

We walked the dirt track
into an open field
where women and children
lifted shocks of wheat
into the mouth
of the thrashing machine
and grain spewed
from its funnel.
Straight across the field
we continued towards
a cluster of small
stucco structures.
Women dressed in the
best they had … with a bindi,
a dot of paint, on their foreheads
and large jewels piercing their nose.
The bride and groom played
ritual games inside the house
to learn to trust one another

since they had met
only in brief moments before this day.
They came out and sat on the dusty earth
of the courtyard encircled by the crowd.
The bride, richly dressed,
veiled so that no one
saw her face was helped
as if an invalid
unable to walk
without assistance.
She would need to learn
to trust these strangers,
her new husband's family.

The groom called to me
in Hindi and I, a stranger,
asked for translation.
"He wants you to see his bride's face."
I was told.
Feeling conspicuous, singled out, and
unsure of what was expected of me,
I crossed the courtyard
in front of everyone,
sat next to the groom
and gazed at his bride's face
as he asked her to pull back
her veil for me.
Ravishing beauty and humility
looked to me for only a moment.

I was speechless a few moments,
then turned to the groom, and said,
"Your wife is beautiful, thank you."
I walked away into the crowd.
Later that afternoon I sat on the dusty ground,
ate from saucers sewn from large leaves
mixing the sauce, rice and beans with my fingers
and scooped them into my mouth.
I laughed as the colorful mixture
dribbled all over me.
I felt at home
in India.

I removed my shoes
bent my knees,
ducked my head
and entered.
The five women and the baby
sat on the bed in the small room,
folding chairs for my companion and me.
I had been there once,
six weeks before,
to assist the young English woman
to begin an English language class.
This was the small end celebration.
The women and I
had enjoyed that first class
and they now had requested my attendance.
We again laughed and gestured

struggling for language to express
our thoughts and feelings
until it was time to leave.
As I stepped out the door to say goodbye,
the older woman stood in the doorway.
Despite Indian taboo,
I was moved to gesture to her
that I desired to give her a hug.
To my surprise she readily accepted a nice big one,
then ordered the other woman
 to come to me for the same.
I felt at home
in India….

Children played in the courtyard,
laughing and talking,
as the young volunteer tried
to get them to sing and dance.
They were shy.
They giggled and laughed
and pushed each other forward.
I jumped out of the doorway
and with my great booming
very flat baritone voice
began to sing
"Zip–a–dee–do–da"
and danced a crazy jig.
"My oh my what a wonderful day…"

"Mr. Bluebird on my shoulder ..."
crazy awkward abandoned movement of all my parts
till I was exhausted and the children delighted.
Suddenly the dancing and singing
rose up from their spirit;
The children were alive with Bollywood.
I felt at home
in India.

The men in detox
filed into the room
forlorn and without smiles.
Some attempted to touch my feet,
to pay their respects to their superior.
I grabbed each one,
gave them a big hug
and a very large smile.
With an interpreter
a few of the men and I exchanged
some conversation.
Most simply stared
as if without comprehension.
After all, I was this large white graybeard
with a long tail of hair
who spoke only English.
They were small dark-skinned inmates
of a repressive "for your own good"
rehab center who spoke Hindi...

Within three days
the men eagerly entered with smiles
and gave me a hug of their own accord.
I felt at home
in India.

I scuffed off my sandals
onto the concrete steps
at the large open door of the temple.
Inside, spacious, dark and cool
with four life-size statues at the far end
lit by oil lamps and candles
attended by a young boy in robes.
I walked within fifteen paces of the statues
of Krishna and Shiva
and their consorts,
stood, unfocused and wondering,
"Why am I here?"
A smallish man entered and stopped
at various places along the side walls
where there were frescoes
that I had not noticed.
He quickly prayed at each
and came to sit on the floor
a few paces in front of me.
Without a word
he motioned for me to sit next to him.
As soon as I did

he raised up
summoning me to follow
and went to the young boy
whose thumb painted a yellow mark
on the man's forehead.
He did the same for me.
The man cupped his hands
as the boy ladled three small amounts
of water into them.
The man immediately
drank some from his hands
and splashed the rest over his head.
I did the same.
The man bowed and went out the door.
I sat on the floor in the middle of that temple
without much comprehension
except
I felt at home
in India.

Identity

He who identifies Himself with Brahma

is the same who has achieved the non-self of Buddha

is the same who has achieved brotherhood with Christ

is the same who has chosen Allah above all

is the same who worships Yahweh

is the same who has great compassion

for the earth and its inhabitants…

Earthen Heroes

The Roof is corrugated steel
the walls are rough red brick
the door is a burlap sack
the toilet is the field beyond
the water is the communal spigot
the heating fuel is cow dung
the labor is by hand and legs and back and head
the morning milk is sought out by children with tin
buckets

Hail! You mighty living who walk tall and with dignity
in beautiful saris and kurtas
There are no motorized vehicles in these hills
all life is slow motion
except for the mongoose and the birds in the air
and even the birds soar easy on the wind

People of the earth know the earth
with human fragility and strong minds
walk steadfast in life and death

Hail! You earthen heroes
the rich, the mechanized, the electronically connected
have much to learn from you
from the earth we have come
to the earth we shall return…every one of us.

Sunday Visitors

As I sit on my veranda at 8 am,
I watch
bright green parrot-like birds
in the trees .
A handsome man
in a clean light green kurta,
a tall beautiful woman
in a red and gold sari
walk through the gate
as if on a Sunday visit.
This man and this woman
begin moving a pile
of heavy stone,
removed from the path,
to be piled neatly
along the courtyard wall.
I would have liked
to take a picture.
No people
would come dressed
so elegantly
to move rocks.
After a short time
I turned my back.
I was embarrassed
for myself,

my life of ease,
my lack of dignity.
Each day I observe
migrant laborers
who live in the hills here.
Each day
I watch them
walk single file along these paths,
whole families
with children in arms
walking to their day's labor.
Late in the evening
I watch them return.
Once again
the man below
creates dung patties
as fuel for cooking and heating.
Once again the mules
and people
ascend and descend these hills.
A baby cries,
a woman washes clothes
on the rocks
near the ditch,
Women carry
heavy stone or soil,
or cement or laundry,
or firewood or animal feed
balanced on their heads.

Sunday morning is like all others.
Their life and work are one.
Their prayer ceaseless.

Indonesia

Jakarta, Bali, Ubud, Semarang, Temanggung,
Rawaseneng, Magelang, Borobudur, Yogyakarta,
Bandung are now places familiar to me…
Terima kasih, sama sama, selamat pagi, selamat siang,
selamat sore, selamat malam are now familiar phrases.
Enak (delicious) has become a favorite word.
Ramadan is now a season that I understand and
appreciate.
Yet, Indonesia unites over 13,000 islands and I have
seen only a small part of two.

                The Indonesian navy man
                a Muslim
                sat one seat from me
                in car number three,
                on the train from Bandung
                to Jakarta,
                stood,
                shook my hand
                and said goodbye
                as I too
                stood,
                pulled my travel bag
                from above
                and followed him
                from the train

onto the platform
into the depot,
eventually losing
his track.
As I stepped gingerly
onto the down escalator,
ever mindful
of my poor knee
and the danger of
a misstep and fall,
and as I allowed
the moving stairway
to carry me down,
I sensed a
commotion
at the top.
An elderly woman hesitated,
afraid of
this people moving
machinery,
afraid to put
her foot down
onto the sliding steps,
afraid of a long
tumble down
a hard shiny
metal hill.
With a waiting crowd behind her,
someone held her tight

as she struggled
with indecision
and balance.
Thankfully,
she mounted
the stairs
and stood solidly
on moving steps.
Suddenly, I realized
no one had stepped
onto the escalator with her.
Where was the press of travelers?
She was alone!
The stairs behind her
were empty.
The stairs between
her and me
were empty.
There was
no one
to assist her
in stepping
to solid ground.
I scrambled up
the ten or twelve stairs
between us
as the stairs continued
their descent
carrying the both of us

to their endpoint.
I gestured to her
to hold on to me
to trust me.
There was no question
of language.
I could not speak
Bahasa Indonesian.
I held her
as she lost her balance
teetering back and fourth,
front to back,
side to side,
till she stepped off
and both her feet
were on a motionless floor.
She gave me a shy
appreciative smile.
There was no question
of language.
I did not speak
Bahasa Indonesian.
A crowd
of onlookers
stopped, stared
and smiled
speaking words
I did not know,
yet, could understand.

The navy man
rushed to me
saying "Thank you".
He took me in tow
to find a good taxi.
As the taxi
careened through
Jakarta streets,
I realized that
this is what
I wanted
from Indonesia:
the opportunity
to give a hand,
earn a smile,
share in the life
of the people.

Spill in Bali

Three days
on beautiful Bali
pampered and solicited
Balinese style.
I stepped off the bus
in Ubud
to meet Mark
at Ary's Warung
walked just twenty paces
down Monkey Forest Road,
turned to check the traffic,
bounced off
a fast-moving motorbike
and…
even as I am in mid-air
watch a young woman
attempt to regain control
as her bike skids from her.
She spills to the pavement.
Dirty and scratched
from my fall
I watch others help her up
check her wounds.
No one speaks.
I follow my heart
go to the young woman

make a deep bow
with sorrow, regret and prayer.
Then I turn and walk away.
No one speaks.
I have lost my enthusiasm
to be a tourist
in other people's lives.
I will leave these good people
and will return only when
some one thinks of
something good
I can do
besides spend money…

The Train

A quiet glide over the land, night and day,
a leisurely pace of contemplation.
Within the slow rocking chambers of quiet
soft people with soft voices in respect,
in respect to the stretch of prairie,
in respect to the majestic mountains,
in respect for the clouds and the sun piercing them,
in respect to the great mass of steel hugging the track
    carrying them to their destination,
in respect to the engineer's advancing and retreating of
the throttle
    sensitive to the demands of a safe journey.

Sliding along the side of the mountain, valley below and
peaks above,
the engine with its following makes a long broad turn
along the contour
as passengers in rear cars, for the first time enjoy the
sight of the engine
    pulling them through mountain passes.

Clouds separate revealing a swath of blue from horizon
to horizon.
Coming down from the mountains the prairie lies before
us, brown and flat
Our train will surely pick up speed

as we leave the treacherous beauty of the mountains.

As we roll across the golden prairie
snow capped mountains frame our view.
Above the mountains a streak of blue
white and gray clouds create a soft canopy for the
earth.

A quiet glide over the land through night and day,
a leisurely pace conducive to contemplation…

At Queen Anne and Mercer

Stop!
Stop thinking.
Put nothing into words.
Put nothing into thought.
Allow yourself to be present.
Allow yourself space
from anxious decisions of the moment.
Forget your history of pleasant as well as hurtful
memories.
Forget your dreams, ideals and future plans.
Surrender yourself to spacious spirit.
Surrender yourself to the present.

I am whole.
I am both deep and spacious.
I am sand, rock, water and air.
I am open and without judgment.
I am compassionate without tension.
I am… I am… I am…

Breathe!
Shanti, shanti, shanti…
Breathe…

Uptown espresso,
your early morning spot for a caffeine wakeup.

A parade of assorted people,
coming and going customers.
The women behind the counter
smile and efficiently fill cup after cup
of custom blended java anyway you desire,
alive sounds of Reggae, chatting friends,
the hiss and growl of the machinery,
the squeak and slam of the screen door,
an awakening for all who enter,
shared energy to begin the new day,
extends beyond the caffeine, aroma
and rich taste of coffee.

The gimped man with cane,
partial paralysis of the left side
including foot, leg, arm and hand
attempted to exit the coffee shop.
His somewhat useless left hand
 slipped off the doorknob.
He shifted his cane to the left
and managed to open the door with his right.
He hobbled to the bus as it pulled away
leaving him standing in the cold…

The unkempt storefront across the street
Papered windows, empty and dark on the inside
proclaimed in large white letters
"Wraps and Smoothies"

Ah! Yes...
Something unwrapped here.
Something rough here.
Gone are the people who peopled the place.
Gone is the dream of "wraps and smoothies."

Swallowing
Swallowing coffee, tea or warm milk
and the pigeons peck at the ground
swallowing crumbs without chewing...

The buses come and go frequently,
hybrid busses with appendages for extra passengers,
trackless electric busses attached to overhead power
and some standard gas fueled...

Young women,
wait at this stopping place
feeding one another
chewing and swallowing one another's talk.

A man and a woman, smoking,
breathe in one another's words.

A lone fellow,
ears filled with headphones
dances silently.

An elderly woman
pecks through her purse.

A bewildered looking old man
nervously shuffles in place.

The bus takes them all away.
The sidewalk is empty except for the pigeons.

Above the Entrance to Club Mercer
A sign across the way proclaims…
"Summer is cancelled? Clarity is overrated."
Considering the weather the sign speaks the truth.
Can there be more to it?
Does it say something about attachment to
expectation?
Allow for mystery!
Sit quietly.
Allow understanding to be wordless.

A Disconnect

Under sunlight and shade trees

The woman reading, the young lady munching

her sandwich,

the young man and woman teasing,

the gulls circling, circling, circling... seeking

crumbs,

the blue sky covers all here with benevolence.

The cell phone rings,

connects this place with other places less

peaceful,

a disconnect between here and there...

Coral on the Beach

The sea is immense,
thousands of miles across,
without light at its great depth.

The sea nourishes a vast array of life forms…even me,
a miniscule being in a community of coral,
a living organism at ocean's shallow edge.

The colony gave me life and I in turn gave life to many.
Linked in a supportive embrace
we became old and brittle.

One day the great and powerful sea
broke us from the colony,
carried our skeleton remains to shore.

On the beach, a conscious being noticed us, carried us
home,
cleaned sand from our frame, acknowledged that we
had lived,
our remains, a bit of the ocean's memory.

Forest Shrouded in Mist

the dew-wet needles of pine and cedar

luscious green ornamented wet sparkle

moist shaggy bark, lichens and moss covering

very old and wise beings…

a soft golden path covered with tamarack needles…

the living trees of the great forest whisper to me

enjoy stillness, live silence, live peace, live enchantment

grow old in wisdom and grace…

The Seed

Having Fallen From the Tree

though the stem be hard and withered,

I ate the meat of the apple,

found the seed.

The seed is me

The apple core remains on my desk:

The apple seed

nourished by apple rot

may have a chance to sprout,

to become a tree

just as I am no longer me.

Old Tree

withered and broken,

has enough seedpods

to populate a forest.

Write of green space, water fountains and squealing children

Grandmother Gingko

Sitting under grandmother gingko,

worrying of words spoken and unspoken,

a chipmunk jumps to a rock nearby,

a man coughs from an open window.

I adjust my position.

The chipmunk runs away.

The window closes.

Sitting under grandmother ginkgo

words are windy gusts that break her branches.

Silence is her strength.

Grandfather Oak

thick and heavy

your weathered face has begun to peel

your leaves more quickly fall

your seed more scarce

the forest owes its life to you

Age

As We Age

our activities may slow

yet, each of us has birthed

a forest of events.

Wind Toys With Treetops

falling leaves laugh and loaf

to the ground of their being.

Pollinated By This Lifetime

my thoughts and actions
provide seed
for the next.

Beauty and trust lay beneath the frozen forest floor
awaiting spring thaw…

Broken Sticks

No more than three inches in length
No more than one-quarter of an inch thick
Dried, brittle, twigs picked up, broken
And piled just eight inches from my crossed legs.

The hot day had burned my skin
The evening breeze refreshes me
The setting sun paints orange,
pink and lavender clouds
Tree shadows draw long across the park.

From the bandstand
Music swirls, tiptoes and dances
Over the heads of the happy, talking, smiling audience,
A few folks rocking and hands clapping, most still and
attentive...

Blankets and people, like colorful flowerbeds,
Spread over rich green grass
I am alone again sitting under grandma Oak...
My life, a pile of broken sticks from the much larger tree
that is me...

A Tree At Fifty

Weather patterns are changing
    as perhaps they ever have
On the edge of the forest
    of a million overlooked trees
From seed to sapling
    you came to be
Roots clasped earth and sucked her breast
Limbs reached skyward to breathe air
    to absorb light
Fertilized by earth and sky you produced
    new leaves and new seed
Your trunk grew thick and heavy
    bearing the weight of all that you could see
Your deeply furrowed surface
    has begun to peel – to reveal
The weakness of age
    your leaves more quickly fall
    your seed more scarce
Tree, I've studied you carefully
    you inspire me
Unique against the bleak landscape
    you stand free
When earth-mother turns over
    and forests are gone
The memories of you, weathered and sun dried,
    will be driftwood for a collector

Yet, memories will not replace the oxygen
    you produce from toxic air
You live at the edge of the forest
    of a million overlooked trees

Songbirds At Sunrise

If I could, I would
implant within your heart sweet voices of songbirds at
                    sunrise
the soft purr of a contented kitten
the cheerful slap of your dog's wagging tail
the nuzzle of a baby lamb
the lick of a fawn
the rustle of Autumn leaves
the silent opening of a flower
the freshening of a light Spring rain
the beauty of winter's white net
the crackle of a campfire under a starlit sky
the gentle lapping of water at lakeside
the warmth of the sun and the cool look of the moon
the aroma of baking bread or fresh apple pie
the giggle of an infant
the smile of a lover
and oh…
so much more…..
within your heart I would implant
If I could, I would
help you understand your great sorrow
by engaging the happiness of little things.

Reunion

I write for you
my long-ago friends,
mates of my youth,
of the unanswered mystery
of our time together

I write for you
not to demonstrate my change
nor your change
nor eschew the years gone by

I write for you…because
those were innocent days for me
as I trust they were for you,
my classmate, my competitor,
my teammate, my chum, my sweetheart

I write for you…because
the boy I was then
is as much me now
and the boy or girl of you
cannot be denied in my heart

I write for you…because
I could not face you today
if I did not understand

our moments together yesterday

I write for you…
no matter our differences
no matter unshared history
no matter challenges,
the successes, the failures,
the joy, the sorrow of years

I write for you as I could not then
I am ready…
to admit my affection for you
to honor your presence in my soul
to embrace you now.

The Knot in My Chest

ones and twos
they trickle through
the door
being opened now
the hall began to swell
the laughter, the chatter
the noise
overwhelming me
the faces squinting
warmly
greeting grotesque me
loneliness
the knot in my chest

Confession

I showered this morning.

In the pool of water at my feet,

a centipede drowned…

Ash Wednesday Friends

"ashes to ashes
dust to dust,"
never a thought of that

the day two six-year-old boys
met, talked and laughed
in a school restroom and
suffered the friendly wrath
of Sr. Lucy

the turtle-necked kid had offered
a bite of his red, juicy apple
never a thought of the giving over a lifetime

the turtle-necked apple boy taught the other
to kick a football
swing a bat
rough-house as friends do
never a thought of the learning over a lifetime

those two boys fighting, arguing, putting
each other to death
never a thought of the pain to be suffered
over a lifetime

those two boys forgiving, forgetting

coming back for more boyhood
never a thought of the loving over a lifetime

those two boys fell sick together
diseased together
never a thought of the prognosis over a lifetime

the turtle-necked, rosy-cheeked, red apple
rough-neck
lost his young strong body
metamorphosed to a sloppy hulk
hauled about by others
while the other boy escaped

the turtle-necked, red apple boy stretching
what he could, grasping, fumbling,
using teeth and chin to survive
struggling to move dead limbs and
accept what has been given
the other boy, the escape artist, full of
movement, sports, travel and admiring
young ladies exciting to the chase
rebellious against conformity and
arbitrary rules

boyhood friends, buddies, now
sitting together, joking, fighting
being friends

climbing steps together,
the one powerful
the other trustful

hitting waffle balls, stalemating chess,
board hockey, electric football and
spring action board games

boyhood friends pass the hours
until one goes his own way
as the other is forced to sit
and sit
and sit
and reflect

the escape artist walked away
in a willy-nilly fashion
steadfast to nothing,
changing, moving, leaving
whatever displeased him

the turtle-necked apple boy
sits and understands…

"ashes to ashes
dust to dust."

Wet Birds Don't Fly at Night

The effort Paul needed to move
I require to be still.
We were given legs that we might learn
to be still
Paul's legs were taken from him
that he might learn to walk.

He sat there, hand to cheek,
elbow rested on the arm of his chair –
large neck of a linebacker, light-haired man,
the withered limbs of a paraplegic
broad buttocks of a man who has spent
most of his life in a wheelchair.
Three eager young boys with athletic bodies sat
listening intently, waiting for the wisdom
of one who might have bested them
if he had not been cut down early in life.
Surely, what was left to this man but wisdom?

He said to the boys nonchalantly,
"Wet birds don't fly at night."
    and again,
"Wet birds don't fly at night."

"What does that mean?" asked the boys.

"Figure it out for yourselves."

"Is that all?"

"Yeah!"

Ten years ago those three boys left that meeting
bewildered, skeptical and amused.
Ten years later, at his death,
the three boys remembered the man and his riddle.

What did he mean? Was he serious?
"Wet birds don't fly at night."

Does it mean all beings have their limitations?
Does it mean that all winging in life must be
tempered by prudent judgment?
These are surely the lessons of a man reared in a
                    wheelchair.
Perhaps it was a chance phrase
- as random as the micro-organism
that fell this man and not others.

Perhaps it was a riddle to chew on
for an entire life,
changing its meaning as life did change
A seed thought that meant nothing
without the soil, the heat, the moisture of a lifetime.
A mantra or focus

from which the reflective life can flower.

The "sage" refused to explain himself.
At the time of his death
the young men simply remembered,
"Wet birds don't fly at night."

Pushing Paul

Walking the courthouse corridor
    déjà vu, pushing Paul across the patio floor
skipping down the courthouse steps
    déjà vu, pulling Paul up the stadium stairs

When too young to understand
my mother's command
"stay by him through thick and thin"

"Wherever you want," I boldly stated,
    no stairs too steep, no path too bumpy,
    no maze too difficult for me
    to navigate a "paraplegic's wheely"

Hadn't seen him in a year
    yet, he was there
    as I pushed someone to overcome a fear

A year ago, we laid him in the ground
    yet he's still around
    as I pull someone from whatever bound

Paul is here in lessons learned:

Help those who cannot move.
Be attentive to their every itch,

disciplined to their call,
never leave them facing a wall.

Arthur

"Gott in Himmel! Du lieber Gott!"
Who is the irreverent old coot?
Like saying, "Who was that masked man?"

Who was he who wandered around his home wearing
    torn pajamas and raggedy slippers?
Who turned down invitations to parties, all
     except his Lord's supper.
Who walked or rode the bus to wherever he would go
    the meat market, the bakery, the Library, the church.
Who stubbornly did everything his own way –
    cooking the meal, washing the dishes, arranging the room,
    making the bed or…loving you.

Who was this solitaire with rosary beads, classical music
    and hundreds of good books to read over and over again?
Who was this Arthur, author of Arturo Potatoes,
    Shrimp Arturo and many gourmet meals?
Who was this man who loved his "objects d'art," and his dogs
    as well as the cats and squirrels and birds of the world?
Who was this man who never looked away, talked straight,
    reminisced and never minced words of the past or present?
How did this city monastic come to have so many acquaintances,
    so many friends, so many who loved him?

"Gott in Himmel! Du lieber Gott!"

...when I was with him,
   he was with me
   and so you...
Arthur gave candy to the children.

In This Cool Month of March

The cool month of March
    when thawing earth releases yellow and purple crocuses
    as sweet signs of Spring's freshening

The cool month of March
    when the sun rises a bit higher each day
    to warm the chilly breeze

The cool month of March
    when earth energies
    awaken from sleep cycle

The cool month of March, after a hard winter,
    when she asked to be carried down the stairs
    to sit in her chair by the window

The cool month of March
    when the early morning sun rays warm the window panes
    brighten her face and shower her in light and energy

The cool month of March
    when she breathed twice and exhaled her last
    returning her breath to the flowers and her soul to God

The cool month of March
    when earth and sky speak in unison

"Do not grieve. We give you life and to life you return. There is no death!"

The Little Man

The nattily dressed little man
    with the large smile
ambled down the restaurant aisle
    shaking hands along the way
then came to sit awhile…with me
"I know you," he said, and I felt important.
"I know the owner here," he said, and I felt proud
    to know him.
"Do you eat here often?" he asked, and I was
    glad to have come this once.
"I come here all the time," he said and I knew
    I would come again.
The little man who shook every hand…
    shook mine,
And said "Goodbye."

Too Soon to Die

Suddenly gone, too sudden to die

> but she did good with her life

Alive, too alive to die

> but she did good with her life

Young, too young to die

> but she did good with her life

Talented, too talented to die

> but she did good with her life

Loving, too loving to die

> but she did good with her life

Undone, too much undone to die

> but she did good with her life

Now, even now

> she does good with her death

Another savior sacrificed

> she bids you

"Do good with your life."

> and remember – she lives.

Widower

She had been planted to flower

for someone

as all flowers do

She blossomed, withered

and died for you

as all flowers do

Her gift lives in your memory

fertile soil for you

to blossom for someone

A Significant Summer

An uninteresting summer
     nothing of significance?

Oh yeah! The bright-eyed seventh grade boy
     who sat in the last seat on the right
     a happy kid who smiled a lot
     straight up in eager anticipation
     died yesterday
     a quirk of fate
     a weak vessel gave way
     drowning his brain
     bio-electrical activity
     stopped.

Now, this is a significant summer for him
     Another savior sacrificed
     for his family, his friends, the world.
In his passing, he asks only this:
     Believe that I yet live
No matter the few years I had with you
No matter the dreams you had for me
     Believe that I yet live
More innocent, more joyful, more in love
     Believe that I yet live
     and you live in me
     and I in you.

A Woman In Red

gaudy red dress
    disheveled red hair
    smeared red lipstick
    cracked red shoes
    and wide ugly tears in her red hose

her arms, legs and hips barely balance
    a too-heavy two-year-old
    having been wrestled from his bed
    before sunrise
    roughly dressed
    carried out the door
    and now clutched in his mother's arms
    aboard a hot, crowded bus
    standing room only

a single parent begins her day
    and the boy cries
    hungry for sleep
    hungry for food
    hungry for affection
    this mother and her son
    cry together

They Say, "She took her own life."

Ahhhhhhhhh yes, yes, yes.............
the life she was given to author
the life that was hers and only hers.
From the spiritual and perfect world
to this relative world she entered with childlike simplicity
as we all have…yet for her and each of us….
something great is at work.
Even though we always were and always will be
a part of God's life and love…
Our relative lives here, in this flesh, are beset
with sufferings of all sorts…
Compassion and forgiveness are our spiritual gifts.
Our suffering is God's suffering.
Our love is God's love.
Our heaven is in knowing this.
Her God-spirit knew from all eternity
that her suffering here would bring new life.
That as she struggled against insurmountable odds
she trusted that there was good in her life.
Did she give up hope? I think not!
She fulfilled her promise………..
She was ready to return to the fountain of her creation
and perhaps, sometime in the future, return again to
this relative world…
Remember… she is alive…………

She can know us with a deep understanding and love.
She is united with the wellspring of forgiveness and compassion.
She wishes that we would grow in the wisdom she now is.

Pray to her: "Matron saint of suffering, grant us peace."

Her Eyes

She squints in the sun.

Her smile pushes her soft cheeks up and out.

Those blushing puffs and ridges of her brow

deepen the valleys of her eyes.

From these mysterious hollows,

dark brown jewels sparkle

with energy of delightful seeing.

My heart leaps from my chest,

splits in two,

falls into her eyes,

Kieran...more than ever...

Oh … Kieran

Oh … Happy Boy

Oh … Warm Smile

Oh … Affectionate Touch

Oh … Quiet and Curious

Oh … Squealer of Delight

Oh … Sharer of High Fives …

Oh … Snuggler …

Oh … Loving Presence

… the short span of your life …

… your gift to us …

What more could you have done?

What more could you teach?

What more could you be?

Could any of us be as much as you?

When I sit and listen …

… you whisper this to me …

"No matter the length of years

I came to love you as you do one another.

I live in you and you live in me as you do one another.

More than ever I understand you.

More than ever I love you.

Feel my love, as you love one another.

Embrace life as you embraced me.

And … remember … more than ever … I live …"

Ash Wednesday's Flower Children

Some time ago…
an Ash Wednesday
when the decorative snow cap had melted
trashing the streets and walks with litter and grit
when the gray sky reflected little light
and the trees remained in death-like dormancy
when my friends and I could not fight the war
or against the war
when we could not fight anyone at all
instead took up fresh flowers and watched them wilt
when we embraced one another
for hope in a despairing time
I remembered then…
the Ash Wednesdays of my childhood
a reminder that my body was earthenware
to be used, worn, cracked, shattered
and reabsorbed by its mother
I wrote then "No man sees my own ash"
a poem for my friends to know
I shared their loneliness, their despair
My poem is lost now…
I could not find it or write it again
Yesterday was another Ash Wednesday
I did not need the dirty thumb of a priest
To smudge my forehead
My smudge is indelibly within my heart

Battle View of the Dead Soldier

My breathing was heavy, fast and deep
and mind without thought
as I ran down the narrow alley
with heavy pack on my back and weapon in hand.
I, like an animal running from its predator,
ran from the bullets that sprayed around me.
I jumped over the limp dead bodies of soldiers, women
and children.
I fled through death and destruction,
through the mud mix of sand and blood
towards the open end of the passage way.
I fled to be safe, to eventually enjoy the comfort of
home.
Suddenly, a sharp pain in the leg, then in the chest and
then in the head,
I began to float up out of the fray of the battle.
I watched as soldiers continued to mutilate one another
as well as the innocent.
I floated with all those dying that day,
men, women and children.
My dead comrades, enemies and I floated together over
the battle.
We all looked down at the scene below and felt pity for
our loved ones who crucified one another.
We floaters, looked at one another as if to say,
"Why have we done this?

This all seems so unnecessary.
Why have we caused so much pain and sorrow?
Why did we not choose to live in harmony and love on
earth as we will in heaven?"
We tried to whisper this to those in the battle to no
effect.
Their minds and hearts were hardened by propaganda.

They could not understand God's will for us, to be
friends and neighbors.
We now sang in unison to the fighters asking them to
simply put down their arms and never fight again.
They were too frightened of one another to listen.
They were locked in "kill or be killed."
We floated away, my comrades, my enemies and I
from that battle scene to speak to our loved ones at
home.
We hoped that by our whispers they would come to
understand.
"In our homes, in our cities and between nations and
ethnic peoples,
stop the fighting and tend to one another's
needs."

Beth Shalom

a point
in time
in space

a forest
perhaps a small plot of earth
a wisp of land at ocean's end

a shelter
a fire on the hearth
bed covers turned down

a window lookout
a rocking chair
hardwood floors

the earth and what we have made from it
stone and wood touched by our hands
penetrated by our vision
transformed by our love

a living presence
our presence in love
in love with one another
in love with all lands and all shelter

Beth Shalom, in you I came to be
that day I walked by your open door
        with never a thought to enter

that day was called struggle
a strange mind I was then
when peace threatened me
as if the trail, the search,
the rocky campsite was all there was meant to be

even now, Beth how long I've known you
my hands twitch fending off
my heart leaps to each precipice
defending with only the fall behind

yet I've been with you
your light had come deep
and swells there

Speckled Path

finger green valleys beneath

    the dew days creamy gray mist

summertime sadness awaiting the fetal hollow hole

    of winter's white wet

escape to the sunlit burning

    of the noontime meadow

a mossy creek splashing down pebbles

trees shadow the sunlit stare

to a speckled earth

speckled water

speckled grass

along the path

In His Own Judgment

yeah! as his hand was betwixt
the space and the plate
yet those sensitive eyes
tuned to every reaction
of brook and flower and foot and wing
his mind so finally set
he gently lay down his mallet
withdrew within the sound
tense time bound
each touch did press
touch sound and resound
until he wept
you thought you had me caught in place
you thought you saw judgment on my face
you thought you had me bound by law
that I myself could not claw
at this sanity that bothers us all
safe in the law that I could not flaw
you're all in error
what you witness you do not see
you never do entirely
in your diversity
only you arrange
nothing evolves no change
react on what you know
believe in what you know not yet

expand yourself to include all things
divide these all to a singular small
or group them tall in a mutual mall
yet a thread weaves through
all we who

Wailing Wall

alone, freely we came to this place

your wailing song echoing the hollow

of your eroded dream

my absorbing ear hiding the me from life

Feather, Fur and Claw

Without feather
>I soar on canvas wings,
>wooden wings, nylon wings,
>steel wings… or whatever works.

Without fur
>I huddle in animal hides, wool,
>cotton, downy quilt… or whatever works.

Without claw
>I dig, tear, mutilate and slice,
>with shovel, scissors, sword and knife
>… or whatever works.

I survive
>on whatever comes to mind.

Habitat

I've been there!

    Where?

To the silent high plains desert
    with dust devils dancing in the distance
    the dry smell of scrub brush, cactus,
        sunlight and stillness.

To the lapping ocean shores' shifting sands
    with water spouts and blue horizon
    the wet salt smell and the call of a gull

To the cool forest green shroud
    with the groaning elephant trees
        and rustling leaves
    the smell of moist living beings erupting
        from compost black earth

I've been there!
    children of the habitat, my kin,
    offspring of the earth
    because I've been there

Alone with the ancient ones.

The Sea, It Is Said

a sad song

shaping souls

swill awashing shores

slipping rocks

melting sand

gathering pebbles

through a wet dimly lit mist

the middle

rolling

in one directionless

middle swell

sinking middle

touching

unceasingly deep

untouched depth

Beneath the Sand

sand wash giving up green living stubble

the silky back of a river gone by

the hint of hidden moisture

beneath ancient earth

the power to grow

Sitting Silently

enjoying quiet sounds

Love and nature mixed in solitude

for all whom I've known

for all whom I will know

Calling, you're calling me forward

around a lake, through the grass

sunlight, butterflies and the

sound of locusts

Silence. A warm gentle summer rain

moistens the earth

encourages seeds to sprout

moistens our faces

Slow motion

every person, every machine, the movements of the sun

all slowed to an unreal dance

Each moment carefully watched

life revealed, secrets learned,

secrets appreciated, no longer hidden

some loved, some loathed

all open to our eyes

The slow dance of life as flowers open

trees spread, you and me

born, growing old and dying

Moments of joy, moments of sorrow

    Love them all

Sundown

crimson and inky blue

day dawn over

the moon rules

Snow Clouds

clouds

then snowfall

earth will again

be fruitful

Desert Mound

crusted mound

mosaic of sand

dwelling place

for organizational man

thank you for the visit

brother ant

Dine'

Attempting to trick the people

    coyote asked this riddle:

If the gift of love came

      from the womb of Mother earth

      and the gift of intellect

      from the loins of Father sky,

      then where did they embrace?

A single voice shouted in response,

    "In the spirit of the people!"

    "In the spirit of the people!"

Coyote laughed and ran away

      to bay at the moon-sky

      from desert-earth

      mourning the loss of spirit-people

Dine'tah

The old man said:

> In his youth his father had warned him, even when
> food is plentiful eat slow and eat little.

> This would harden him for hard times.

> Today, the young men stretch their bellies with
> fast foods each time they eat.

The old man said:

> In his youth his father stripped him in the snow,
> ordered him into the sweathouse –
> "Pour water over the hot stones .feel
> the generous warmth penetrate to the bone,
> breathe the vapors of life
> into the cavities of your body,
> cleanse the spirit."
> Roughly pulled from this cocoon
> into knee-high snow,
> he was forced to run for many miles
> thrashed with a switch by his father.

This would harden him for hard times.

Today, the young men turn on the warm shower
and wash a river of precious water down a drain
cleansing their mirror images while their spirit
waits.
Those young men leave the warm shower to a warm
room, to a warm car, to a warm school to be taught by
the warm breath of strangers.

The old man said:

In his youth his father and other young men tied
a sack of pemmican at their hip and together ran
one hundred and more miles to a Pueblo village
stopping only to drink at a clear stream and eat
pemmican. Without weapons they stole horses.
and rode home in song and praise

They were hard men for hard times.

Today, the young men lock themselves in factories
chained to machines and endless repetitive action
under a man-made light leaving them tired and
discouraged at the end of the day.

The old man said…
    The old days were better…

A Dry Wind

a warm dry wind has swept the land

the sun glistens off the few puddles

abandoned by the receding snow

the crystal lace has gone now

leaving the barren skeleton

of the deep down things

like the self of me retracting

into the darker passageways

your words have melted my

crystal self

leaving only

a skeleton statue

Oh! Spring come quickly before I rot.

A Jack Rabbit

a jack rabbit, a meadowlark, a wash filled with water

around the arid valley

colorful rock and green pinion-covered mountains

around the arid valley

a few scattered huts squat and swelter

listen to the rhythmic rush of legs against sagebrush

feel the sun beat down, face burned, mouth dry

eyes looking for something to see

walking silently, searchingly

Who will walk with me?

Empty "I"

Flesh, muscle, cartilage, bone

    become human carnage

Healthy organs become diseased

Cells metamorphose into destructive growth

The graceful and athletic become paraplegic

Intelligent and bright become brain dead

Virile become weak

Young become old and memory fades

Personal forms change… and… What remains of

    the "I" that I speak?

I was the zygote, the embryo, the fetus…

I was the infant, the toddler, the young child…

I was the pre-pubescent, adolescent, young adult…

I was the middle-aged, old-aged, corpse, the dust,

the dust that cannot be distinguished from the

soil which sustains plant life.

What remains of the "I" of whom I speak?

…Yea… a spiritual entity whose changing form

prevents me from knowing myself

or… whose changing points to an empty "I"…

unchanging and entirely spiritual.

No matter the conditions of your life, you are,

at all times, pure spirit hitching a ride

on the material universe… enjoy the journey.

My Desert

The desert is a silent state of being

wherein no one calls my name.

No one knows my name.

I have no role to play in human affairs.

No identity.

The moment within is perfectly attentive

to the moment without.

History is my demon.

You cannot see my desert.

I cannot see yours.

Drawn

Why am I drawn to desert hogans
  and not presidential houses?

Why am I drawn to forests of trees
  and not church cathedrals?

Why am I drawn to grassy meadows
  and not city parks?

Why am I drawn to splashy creeks
  and not mall fountains?

Why am I drawn to the ocean's edge
  and not the sports stadium?

Why am I drawn to hand-made
  and not machine made?

Why am I drawn to other lifestyles
  and not the American dream?

Why am I drawn out of harmony
  and not able to melt in?

Why am I drawn to stillness
  as the world rushes from me?

Earth Me

Stars upon the sky of me

Salt within the sea of me

Sand upon the beach of me

Trees within the wood of me

Moss upon the tree of me

Life within the earth of me

Saving Grace

Souring savior sacrifice

shaping shut eyes

SHOUTING skin-lit

heating

I holler, "be cool man!"

The Hearer Who Is No Hearer

the school that is no school

the government that is no government

let us not bind ourselves

by the definitions of our minds

perfection is "no definition!"

My Chosen Path

My chosen path
   Unlike yours
Treads downward into caverns within.
This path has no room for two abreast.
   Very few have gone before,
   none are expected to follow.
Signs left behind
   for those who cross the path
   reveal whatever was learned
   leaving for others the decision
   whether it was worth the trouble

Bus Stop

While I waited a short time for an
  air-conditioned bus to deliver me to
  an air-conditioned office for a day of
  quiet, unpressured paperwork,

I was attacked at that bus stop by a swarm
  of small flies – the first time such has happened.

It is enough to make a spoiled man angry!
  Not withstanding the maggots, lice and
  horse flies crawling into the eyes, ears,
  nose and mouth of belly-bloated children
  waiting at the bus stop of death.

Early Morning

Fog and mist in early morning
  fill the valleys with invisible peaks

Sun rays pierce the gray air
  and all things are barely there

We who walk the city in early morning
  through a park, across a bridge
  down a narrow street

Some of us walk afraid

Some reflect on the stories housed behind
  closed doors

Some watch the dog foraging or the cat
  hunting

Some note the flowers about to bloom
  and trees freshening to spring

Break the Silence

Whistle…Break the Silence
intrude on my private thought
you blundering ass!
sitting in my back yard, my small woodland world
a neighbor turns his radio out an open window
a motorcycle blasts down the street
a mother screams at her children
gentle thoughts turn to angry words
the gentle and silent are extinct
loud noise-making people rule the earth

Who Rides the Bus

The bus system says,
        "The number of passengers is declining".
Who will ride the bus?

For ten years I rode with the regulars.
Occasionally we chatted, yet
        I never knew from where they came
        or where they go.
        They didn't know me either.
Who rides the bus?

The tight-lipped over age underachieved
        low-level administrator
        going nowhere;
The single parent struggling with
        job, home, children – exhausted
        going nowhere,
The grandpa-ma, whose children have
        moved from town,
        going nowhere,
The young teen forced across town
        to a foreign education
        going nowhere,
The well-dressed store clerk reading
        her passion book,
        pretending to go somewhere.

All aboard!
Looking down upon the soft
    warm insides of private
    commuter-mobiles,

Watching wealthy executives
    disembark from
    washed limos,

Gazing over the heads of
    the prep school kids
    chauffeured to school by dad.

Viewing as through a TV screen
    the comfortable quiet life ,
    bundles of people sharing a ride.

Stone silent the bus herd
    sits in rows staring ahead
    and occasionally to the side
    through mud-spattered windows
    at a gray world.

Behind The High Walls

Prisoners look up.

Crystal blue and puff ball clouds
    blown by high-up winds
    and the hawk circling, gliding,
    feeling the flow of the updraft

The prisoner in the dry dirt
    at the corner of the yard
    looks up

The air he breathes is the same
    as the free man's
    the sky he watches is the same
    as the free man's
    the dirt, the cloud, the hawk
    all universally the same

Suddenly, a feeling of relief
    a gentle smile
    a surge of spirit

The prisoner feels "ok"
    akin to all free spirits
    this space, this sky
    is this man's home.

Cut Brass

cut brass

fired by a violent forge, hand pounded

    mellowed in sunlit glare

a silver thread slowly heated of a constant flame.

    softly blown cool by a gentle breeze to a graceful

    form untouched

they met in night to love

without touch an embrace

he leaps high bounding from rock to ledge

    slicing the air, body sensitive, alert, aware

she rises slightly moving effortlessly, tossed

    body relaxed, gentle, jest

thoughts touch

two strain to listen

leap to tell all thought need be said

reason laid bare against feeling

drawn back, felled

love suppressed

The Graduate

When the first of the clan graduated
    How did they celebrate?
    gifts of joy
    nothing else
    so little did they have

The second generation saw so much more
    had so much more
    great parties
    many little pleasures
    surprises for the graduate

Now, the third, worldly wise
    powers and freedoms
    unheard of by ancestors
    more than any before
    jobs and dreams and appetite
    that no family can provide

    Yes, the young will dare
    and the family will applaud
    Will they hear our joy, our fear?
    Will they see us from afar?
    Realize who we are?
    Will they see their family tree?

Bread and Butter

bread, bread, bread and butter

toast, cereal, coffee and milk

sausage, eggs, cheese and the animals we kill

beef steak, pot roast, hamburger, veal and chickens

with their heads lopped off

fish with their bellies split open

vegetables plucked while young

fruit ripped from the tree

beer, wine, booze of all sorts

money and gluttony

TVs, radios, stereos, autos and variety shows

clothes, wigs and lovely legs

eyes, ears, nose, mouth

filled, stuffed, plugged with

money and gluttony

A Swift On A Trip

A swift on a trip

alone with a tone

a boot on a hoot

a tray out flat

spark

a bite is worse than a bark

Kites

one, two, three, four kites

yellow, green, red against blue

one sways, another soars

a third, not near the other two

does tricks for you.

Creation Tickles Earth

creation tickles earth

      slides down sideways

      trucking the road

         forming roots and trees,

         flowering

         enjoying

         the flight

         of happy

         little things

Sledding

black boy sledding

      snow covered turning white

white boy sledding by

      all white feeling wet

Digging Through the Snow Cover

black brick frame

garbage can gutter

dark marked adolescence

blended bleak brick

hands tactile stretch and touch

sidewalks

porch rails

telephone poles

climbing cement walls

Soar Wing-ed

soar wing-ed

black brother

from the crushing down

into peak-ed light eye

wind center calm

wings black brother wings

free at last

eternal souls winging

while other men sleep

Dissent

I hunger for beauty

as you hunger for order.

Would we be better companions

If neither were so insistent

upon perfection?

Waves

low lines…moving…circling

into waves past beautiful

outward bound to lengths beyond

the sea breaks in…washes under

lapping, lapping, lapping

the shoreline…with huge heavy hands

This Small Seed

love reflex

tripped in echo

from my parents

My Life Has Breadth

to the stars

to the depths

my life is free

to wander

as it pleases me

Like A Spear

Like a spear in the hand of the Spirit

Piercing men

Loosening love

Illuminating creation

Never Bind Self

Let us never bind ourselves

by the definition of our mind.

Let us never define ourselves.

My Mother

when I remember her now

she is the silent woman

whom I didn't know

who birthed all the world

that is mine

Child's Kiss

charm and light

sweeping flight

through airy mist

a child's kiss

Beginning

an upending roar

began man's chore

foraging through

this earthly milieu

Penny King

a one-penny king

    with a one hundred penny moon

and stars blazing above

    would I had one hundred penny more

to satisfy my love

The Telephone

thin miles of wire

a tangle of twisted line

a barbed fence

distance distorting

everything we say

The Donkey's Dilemma

did you ever see a donkey
sit on an egg placed by an owl
would that he had the wit
to hush
those who laughed
who called him foolish
if by chance
the egg stayed whole
only he would know

To Exist

to exist is to bow

it is to how

yet

are you a cow

or a plow

thee

see

thee

be

We Dinosaurs

As magnificent as they may have been

dinosaurs did not survive.

They were meant for only a period,

a transition of time.

In their time, lords;

yet, in time, extinct.

For some remote reason

we could not be, if dinosaurs had not been first.

Honor the dinosaur and remember

the future could not be if we had not been first.

The First Flower Picked By Children

bouquets gifted to their parents
an excellent tasting and nutritious salad herb
a beginning for a delicate light wine
some say, when we fail to smile
the dandelion keeps it safe for us

This wonderful, silent, forgiving plant
is in this society considered a weed,
an unwanted, unruly intruder
a scourge on neat lawns and gardens
a trespasser, a criminal
to be dug out and destroyed

I'm afraid this action says more
about this culture than it says
about the dandelion and remember…

When you are made to feel unwanted
thou art the dandelion,
a flower cherished by children
a tasty and nutritious herb
a beginning for new wine
a place for someone to find a smile.

Apple Pie - A La Mode

An overcast late summer day,
a hint of autumn in the air,
the last vacation day of the season.

We sit by the pond with nothing
    what-so-ever to do.
The nine year old climbs into the apple tree.
She begins to pick the nearly ripe.

Mother says, "Let's make apple pie."
Father snatches the paring knife.
He peels and chips away at those wormy apples.

An hour later, the crust had been rolled,
    stuffed with slices of apple,
    sprinkled with sugar and cinnamon,
and the fresh, sweet aroma of baking
fills everyone with anticipation of
    pie – a la mode.

After supper, large hunks of flaky crusted pie
    are wedged onto plates
    oozing syrupy juices
    heaped with vanilla ice cream

Within a few minutes the pie is gone,

the afternoon is history.
That very next morning
the routine rooster will crow
"Back to school, back to school."

July Fourth Feast

For my Mother, Father, Aunt Emmy, Uncle Skin, Uncle
Joe, Aunt Lil, Aunt Mary, Uncle Jake, Aunt Doris, Aunt
Dorothy, Uncle Al,
my brother, sisters and all my cousins…
People of Bohemia by ancestry and marriage
Working the earth, people gathered on the farm
Women preparing food
Men enjoying beer and horseshoes
Children playing in the hayloft

Each year the greatest Fourth of July feast of all time
Bellies full
The men sleep under the cigar tree
The women quietly converse in the shade
The children wander off into the knee-high corn
That evening the great bonfire is set ablaze
The accordion comes to life
The people sing, dance, tell stories, laugh and talk
Cheerful people sharing their lives
     Good stewards to the land and to one another.

Desert Life

The desert is barren and dry

only to the clouded eye

It seldom rains there

yet scant moisture

allows plants to grow

nourishing snakes, birds and mammals.

The desert blossoms with life.

Only the barren eye sees no beauty

Amidst the sand and rock.

Black Bug

A tiny multi-legged black bug
crosses a large boulder
indifferent to the noonday heat.
This remnant of ages ago
ekes out a scant existence
on this barren plateau.
This small creature is perfectly adapted
like a person who finds joy in existence
without much stuff.........

May I Go To The Desert With You?

May I go to the desert with you?
Where silence and stillness
Intensify our desire,
Bless our lovemaking.
We are not alone.
The rocks whisper
Our conscious divinity.
The sand welcomes our bodies' touch.
Sage and cactus smile and approve.
Gecko, snake, and spider look in awe.
Coyote howls in joyful anticipation.
Mountains protect us from afar
And reflect our union to the universe.
Clouds billow with delight.
The moon climaxes with intimate knowing.
Stars beckon eternal bliss.
We embrace and affirm the oneness of the universe…

Michael Awaits Michael

Meet on 4th and Central at 5 PM.
It is now 4:31 PM.
The Harley parade has passed.
Fewer people trickle from the grandstand.
A bearded old man, looking as if
he ought to be driving a huge Harley,
pedals past on an old bicycle.

Young men behind me speak animatedly
of their mile-high experiences.
In what direction do we examine ourselves?

The sun is warm and the shade cool
on this cloudless Friday afternoon
in Great Falls, Montana.

The library was busy.
The coffee shop crowded.
I sit here on the street, waiting for the next moment,
till I am picked up by Michael.

Antique Goblet

Imagine if you will a vessel of clay

A hollow filled to the rim

Chipped edge, cracked stem

Drought-dry, worn by the years

Should the designer destroy this vessel?

Or should it be taken to his lips

To kiss all those who drank from it

Then lift it to a higher place

To honor its antiquity

The Ballad of Moo Ching, Brother to the Wild Goose

Who Follows the Wayward Wind?

Born... ahhhhh...

...The insignificance of that when there is no birth and no death.

Loving humble family, down to earth.

Father, mother, siblings, friends and relatives, the salt.

He walked. He flew...

Away! Away! Away!

Returning, returning, returning as the circling wind blows.

Sitting a spell ... yet everyone knows.

He will be going, going, gone.

To the mountains, to the plains, to the sea.

A gleaner, a gatherer, who leaves behind

The story of his life.

For the Moo Ching he does, he is kind.

This Woman

Who has not been served by this woman?
Who has not known her insistent "I love you!"?
Who has not experienced her pull that brings your
return?
Who has not heard her strong advice?
Who has not been welcome at her table?
Who has not had her rush to help or to heal?
Who has not felt her grief for others who grieve?
Yes, motherhood and servant hood!

Has she ever allowed anyone to wash dishes alone?

Noted Authors

You speak of noted authors

who are indeed held in esteem

by all others, except I say by me,

for within my own heart I look

to see with deepening curiosity

and record with utmost secrecy

feelings that arise in me

for no one sees just how I do

nor reacts in my way

perhaps someone will

read me some day

The Journey..........

1, 32, 44, 564, 2, 10, on,
at, 5, 85, 64, 69, 72, 83, 99, 100,
for the time, 23, 42, 84, 84, 84, 83, 72,
cat, dog, tree, and me, 22, 16, 5, 8, 56, 29,
to the store, 23, 9, 400, 5000, 78, 3, 27, 560,
take me with you, 5, 56, 59, 34, 39,
jump high, 11, 17, 97, 85, 67, 73, 20, 10, 11,
dog day, do little, don't try, 23, 24, 785, 342, 962,
time is now, talk to me, be nice, jump for joy,
36, 82, 91, 1000, 1001, 5000, love that music,
read me, 2, 5, 8, 1, 2, 3, 4, 5, 6, 7, 8.
lunch, soup, tea, coffee, breakfast, apple pie, fry
bread,
panchatantra.

To focus on that which we know is easy,
    familiar and useful…
To focus on that which we do not know is
    to open windows beyond our experience.

9 786028 397001